Angkor

Marc Riboud

Angkor
the serenity of
buddhism

Introduction by Jean Lacouture
With essays by Jean Boisselier and Marc Riboud
Photograph captions by Madeleine Giteau

Thames and Hudson

This work presents a photographic evocation of
Angkor which reflects a personal feeling rather than
any special aptitude for description or
archaeological expertise.

M.R.

Translated from the French *Angkor: Sérénité bouddhique* by Ruth Sharman

This edition © 1993 Thames and Hudson Ltd, London
© 1992 Imprimerie nationale Éditions

Printed and bound in France

Contents

A Suspended Tragedy

At one time this was virgin forest. Then men invaded it and tamed it; they carved stone temples here as places to invoke and worship their gods. Over the centuries, the forest endeavoured to exact its revenge, smothering the temples and the stone effigies in its vast embrace. The men hacked back the forest and salvaged their stone monuments; but whether their actions pleased the gods themselves is another matter. . . .

Angkor attracts vast hordes of people, who come in the hope of receiving the Buddha's gift of peace. Many come in vain, experiencing instead the despair which is the by-product of a history which, right up to the most recent times, has been so tragic that it seems to have left its mark on the very stones and trees.

No monument or beauty-site is so sublime that the circumstances surrounding our first visit fail to affect the way we remember or imagine it. The pyramids which Bonaparte first glimpsed through a haze of gunpowder and the dust-clouds raised by the Mamelukes' charges must have looked rather different to the Vicomte de Chateaubriand, gazing at them in the distance when he passed by, seven years later, on his way to a happier meeting in Granada. Nor may we suppose that the novelist André Malraux viewed Angkor (which figures prominently in his *The Royal Way*) with the same eyes as the Catholic diplomat Paul Claudel, who visited the place as a tourist under the guidance of curator Jean Commaille.

How can anyone think of Angkor in an aesthetic sense, even after reading the works of George Coedès or Maurice Glaize, or, preferably, the comments of Paul Mus, which accurately situate it in its sacred context, if their first glimpse of the place has been clouded by the devastations of war and the conflicts of a troubled history?

Such an experience reveals a place whose memories are essentially tragic. It is an experience with which Marc Riboud's photographic interpretation remains at odds, however faithful his images, however carefully they avoid the purely 'decorative' or aesthetic in their portrayal of a serenity that is for ever threatening to disintegrate. The contemporary historian invited to introduce and comment on those images remembers something altogether more sombre, a fruit altogether more bitter; he continues to hear, as a distant echo, the cries and tears and imprecations of a nation torn apart by war.

Riboud faithfully conveys the outward aspect of Angkor today, and hints at something more. His sensitive interpretation, backed by a firm understanding of the historical issues, allows a certain tension to come through. And yet, behind the grey stones and the giant trees, behind the smooth-skinned faces and the gentle gestures, lurk so much wild fury, so many centuries of bloodshed, such recent horrors. . . .

In August 1946, an old Dakota was flying through a cloud of butterflies over the 'temple-city' of Angkor. A twenty-four-year-old reporter sat with his face eagerly pressed up against the window while memories of an earlier visit, to the Colonial Exposition in Paris fifteen years previously, came rushing back to him. He saw looming out of the forest, a little darker now than in his childhood memory of them, the 'five pineapples fringed with flames' which had once made Claudel smile, and the plane almost brushed them with its wing as it flew over.

I was that reporter. And already, by force of circumstance, the huge shrine struck me less as a place of worship than as a stake in a power game. If our squadron was zooming in like a flight of helmeted *garudas*, it was not in order to transport pilgrims to Angkor, or indeed disciples of Henri Parmentier or Henri Marchal; we were flying in, with a warlike drone of engines, to repel a new threat to the Khmer kingdom from its insatiable Thai neighbours: the Bangkok army had only just restored the treasures it had looted from Phnom Penh, but now, giving way to a change of heart, had planned a new raid.

Scattered across the forest around the western Baray like so many giant waterlilies were the parachutes belonging to Colonel Bollardière's commandos, who had dropped over Angkor in order to drive back the Thais. I had been commissioned by the journal *Caravelle* to report on this tutelary action by the French 'protector'. On first arriving, on the paved western peristyle, instead of yellow-robed monks I saw men in camouflage gear; instead of parasols, sub-machine-guns; and instead of chanting, I heard warning shouts. I did not catch sight of the aggressor but what I did see, rather damaged by the crossfire, was the temple-pagoda in the heart of the forest.

One night, twenty years later, an unusually tall man strolled across those same paving stones between two ranks of torch-bearers and caparisoned elephants. The saffron robes of a thousand Buddhist monks stationed in the temple niches glowed as the torches passed by. At the tall man's side walked a plump little figure who gesticulated so violently he seemed to have four arms instead of two, like the god Vishnu. The tall man was Charles de Gaulle, his companion and host Prince Norodom Sihanouk. But the participants of this scene had not gathered for the purposes of worship, or tourism, or diplomatic protocol. Far greater issues were at stake: issues of war and peace. If the general, who the previous day at Phnom Penh had delivered a speech that has gone down in history, failed to relax the grip of war in this sacred region, Cambodia, as everyone knew, would plunge headlong into a conflict that had little hope of resolution. The torches cast their strange and beautiful light over everything: the banyan trees and the monks' saffron robes glowed and the monks' impassive copper-brown faces shone with a soft radiance; the *apsaras* seemed to dance on the bas-reliefs; the visitor's long nose seemed to lengthen and the *Samdech-Euv*'s gestures to multiply. Yet the fact remained: this peaceful scene was no more than the prologue to a tragedy whose horror no one could have fully anticipated.

Twenty years on, the horror had expanded into cataclysm. Which of those present on the night of 1 September 1966, aside from the prince with the commanding voice, remained now to bear witness? Terror reigned once more in the city of a million leaves, among the temple-tombs, the bodhisattvas, the *apsaras* and the guardian spirits of the paths and sacred lakes. But this time it was not the Javanese with their narrow dugouts sweeping down on Jayavarman II, or the quarrelsome Chams looting Suryavarman II's capital, or the plundering Thais laying waste to the holy city of the 'Leper King', or even the hated Vietnamese Yuon trampling Siva's dwelling-place; now it was a handful of Khmers possessed by the insane dream of transforming the temples of the god-kings into factories for manufacturing men without identities, for ever enslaved to Angkar-Leuh, the Power Above, who laughs at the notion of gods and domestic comforts.

Somewhere in Angkor – though I have been unable to discover the exact location of the crime, since the guides have been either unable or too frightened to reveal it – my old friend René Puissesseau was murdered by a group of these bloodthirsty utopians, who regarded any Westerner (Paul Mus and George Groslier included) daring to step on Khmer soil as a filthy intruder worthy of punishment.

The Khmer Rouge attacked with clubs and pickaxes all those who refused to leave the temples, either hacking or beating them to death. They strangled or suffocated or cut the throats of those who made a living collecting birds' nests, or fishing in the Baray, or gathering mangoes – 'stealing what belonged to the people', as they called it. A reign of absolute terror engulfed what was once a haven of piety and tranquillity, and the authors of the terror were the sons of those selfsame women who may be seen meditating before the Buddha in the eastern gallery, their heads humbly bent, their hands joined together in prayer.

Angkor, once glorious, is now a tragic place which peace can only reconquer, if 'conquer' is the right word, in a slow and solemn fashion, as Marc Riboud's images suggest – images that have been assembled in this very spirit, as a humble ceremonial, celebrating prayer and the renewal of life. And yet, the armed men are still in evidence: we see them mingling with the groups of women shading themselves from the sun, loitering at the lakeside, crossing paths with the monks who walk with heads bent in quiet reflection.

My wife and I had visited Cambodia in its honeymoon years, and we now wondered naively how such a paradise devoted to the teaching and precepts of the Blessed Enlightened One could be disrupted by war and violence. How could they affect the fishermen of Tonle Sap or the ploughmen of Sisophon or the monks who recited the temple prayers?

We learnt the answer well before the great storm broke, even before the slide into war that began at the end of the sixties, and before the anti-Vietnamese pogroms of 1972. Paul Mus was astounded by our naivety. 'Do you really imagine', he asked, 'that a people who, under successive rulers, have been responsible for creating such splendours, for digging these canals, building these huge temples, conquering and destroying Champa, dominating the entire Indochinese peninsula, have always been a smiling people? Believe me, building is like conquering: to achieve either you have to be violent. The Khmers are violent by nature, and they can be truly ferocious. One day you'll see the explosion.'

Some time later, Bernard Groslier wrote: 'The Khmer carries deep in his heart a vague and brooding fear, the terror felt by primitive man in the face of a hostile world. Out of his apparent unconcern, sudden violence can erupt and flashes of disconcerting cruelty – the brutal blaze of passion.'

This blaze of passion, which Prince Sihanouk compared for us with the Malays' murderous *amok*, has become an unquenchable fire, implacably fuelled during the last thirty years by the men in the employ of Saloth Sar, or Pol Pot, as he is otherwise known. Born into a wealthy élite which owed its allegiance to the royal palace, he was trained in the 'imperialist' schools and is responsible for inventing one of the most inhuman systems of social control the twentieth century has known.

Other visitors, from farther afield, have intuited that feeling of terror, that foretaste of disaster, which lurks behind Angkor's sublime sense of order and calm. In the 'temple crushed in its utter abandonment' by 'the secret violence of the plant-life', André Malraux discovers that 'something inhuman' which 'brings to bear on the rubble and the all-consuming plants, themselves mesmerized like petrified animals, a terror which [protects] with the potency of a corpse those figures whose age-old gestures reign over a court of centipedes and wild beasts crawling among the ruins. . . .'

What the author of *The Royal Way* feels is simply the existential anguish for which Jean-Paul Sartre so admired him – even though he was later to provide a more daring aesthetic interpretation for *The Voices of Silence*, those whispers of the forest inhabited by stones and insects and gods.

It is as a Christian that Paul Claudel expresses his horror in the face of this Panic celebration of the spirits of shade and plant and forest. It is an astonishing revolt on the part of this epic inventor of storm-tossed galleons and conquistadors, Jesuits and separated lovers – a revolt against what Claudel describes as 'those nocturnal shrines where bats fly in and out . . . reeking with a smell that is both sweet and vile (probably emanating from their droppings). Those closed jewels that delight from a distance, with their worm inside, that blasphemous ostentation.' The charges then become more precise: 'Was this perhaps the Devil's own temple before me, and had the earth refused to support it? Was this then the reason for the attackers' extraordinary rage, the fury they unleashed on all the idols? . . . Down below was the world of water and mud, of grubs, fish, turtles and crocodiles; up above were the infinite numbers of *apsaras* dancing around, floating skywards like mosquitoes, like air bubbles.' Such, then, are the feelings of this Christian poet looking down in a blind fury on 'that accursed temple'. 'Angkor', he concludes, 'is one of the most accursed, the most evil, places that I know. I was ill when I returned from there, and the account I had written of my journey was destroyed by fire. . . .'

In the ninth century, Jayavarman II chose the Kulen plateau, west of the Great Lake, as the site on which to build the capital which would unify Kambuja of the Land (southern Laos, upper Leuh and southern Annam) and Kambuja of the Water (the lower Mekong basin, now southern Vietnam). He liberated his people from the rule of the Javanese, 'those cannibals, living off foodstuffs even more horrible than the flesh of corpses, fearsome people, emaciated and jet-black, who arrived in dugouts' and who cut off the heads of Khmer kings, 'putting them on platters', and he defied the arrogant Siamese. A period of glory began for Angkor, but Jayavarman cannot have imagined that his people would enjoy peace for long: with the Chams on one side and the Siamese on the other, and with occasional threats from the Burmese in the west and the Chinese and Vietnamese in the north, the future for the Khmers in the time of Charlemagne promised to be an unstable one. It was. However imposing their civilization may seem to us now, with its noble aspirations towards Buddhism and Brahmanism, the Khmers experienced a succession of tragedies comparable to those that rocked Carolingian Europe and the Christian world during the time of the Crusades.

While monasteries and cathedrals were springing up everywhere from the Rhine to the Tagus, on the Kulen plateau and the west bank of the Tonle Sap magnificent temples were being built as monuments to the grandeur and ambitions of the Khmer god-kings. Towards AD 1000, Suryavarman II, the 'Protégé of the Sun', built the city-temple of Angkor Wat. We call it a 'city-temple', but was it in fact a temple, a palace, a fortress or a tomb? One thing it was not was a palace; it had nothing to compare with Versailles or the Escorial. Nor was it a fortress. It had no surrounding walls or dykes or moats, nothing to identify it in any way with the original Louvre or the Castel Sant'Angelo. Such a massive stone structure could, if the occasion arose, stave off an attack; but this was not the purpose that lay behind its conception, any more than it was in the case of Cluny or the Vatican.

As with the majority of Angkor's architectural and sculptural masterpieces, the Angkor Wat edifices served as both shrines and royal tombs; their purpose was not as dwelling-places but as places of worship where preparations could be made for the forthcoming interment of the god-king. They were occasionally monasteries, but not in the sense of housing a monastic community and servicing its, albeit frugal, day-to-day requirements, as in the case of modern temples. Their sole purpose was related to worship and funerary rites.

We can draw a tentative parallel with the Egyptian monuments from the time of the Pharaohs. When he first arrived in the Nile valley, Jean-François Champollion spoke of the 'palace' of Karnak, but he rapidly registered his mistake and henceforth referred to the building as a 'temple'. But can we go so far as to compare the god-kings of the Asiatic jungle with those of the African valley, Siva with Ptah the Founder, Vishnu with Thoth the Wise, Brahma with Amun the Supreme, Buddha with Osiris the Compassionate? Both Asia and Africa have their temple-mountains designed as burial-places for their god-kings. And anyone who has seen both the gigantic faces of the Bayon Lokesvara and the Abu Simbel colossi cannot fail to draw a comparison between these two great architectural wonders with their superhuman proportions.

It is also tempting, although they are separated in time by twenty-five centuries, to see a parallel between the lives of the last two great sovereigns of the Nile and the Kulen. Great conquerors and builders alike, Ramesses II and Jayavarman VII seemed to bring all the collective power of their respective civilizations to bear on one last mighty and ruinous effort to crown the glorious achievements of their reigns. Ramesses' great triumph, the Ramesseum, was the supreme expression of the art of the New Empire, while Jayavarman's Bayon marked the practical and symbolic culmination of that jungle theocracy which the Khmers had introduced to the world. For Jayavarman's distant successors, after centuries spent cowering in terrified submission, this 'lost' city, now rescued from the creepers, leaves and moss under which it had long lain buried, was to represent the very heart of their renaissance.

The king who built the Bayon is the most intriguing figure in Khmer history, appearing to embody that blend of compassion and violence that typifies the people of Cambodia, setting them apart from any of the civilizations and cultures from which they have drawn their inspiration, including that of India.

For many years, historians and archaeologists argued that the famous statue of the so-called Leper King, crouching 'Javanese fashion' (with one knee raised) on a burial-mound on the terrace of Angkor Thom, represented Jayavarman VII. The carved sandstone eroded by lichen corresponded to what was known of the king's appearance, and suggested the characteristics of that most pathetic of medieval maladies. Yet one might as soon suppose the Smiling Angel of Rheims to be a portrait of Saint Louis.

George Coedès, for his part, had no difficulty in demonstrating that the famous statue had nothing whatsoever to do with the seventh of the Khmer kings styled 'Protégé of

Victory' (Jayavarman). According to Coedès, the two minute fangs jutting out at either corner of the statue's lips, together with the hair falling around its shoulders, identify the figure as a demon – and Jayavarman, for all that he was a megalomaniac, never claimed demoniacal powers.

Jayavarman VII's life, however, provided a rich vein of epic interest. The principal source is a stele translated by Coedès, from which we learn that in 1177 'Jaya Indravarman, king of the Chams and as arrogant as the demon Ravana . . . brought his army over in chariots and attacked the country of Kambu, which is like the Heavens', and that the Cham fleet, guided by a Chinese castaway, sailed up the Mekong river as far as Tonle Sap and sacked the wealthy but defenceless Angkor, where a usurper had claimed the throne. It was at this point that Jayavarman appeared on the scene, waged a number of battles against the Chams, both at sea and on land (one of these is magnificently illustrated on a Bayon bas-relief), liberated his country and claimed the throne, restoring the capital to its former glory. As one of the stelae placed at the corners of the Angkor Thom wall expresses it, 'The city of Yasodharapura, like a young girl of good family, a fitting match for her husband, for whom she burns with desire, crowned with a palace of precious stones and clothed, as it were, by its ramparts, was wedded to the king for the purpose of procreating the happiness of all beings; and the wedding, which took place under the canopy of his unfurled glory, was accompanied by a magnificent feast.' The city which the king is said to 'marry' is Angkor Thom.

While waging war against his unruly eastern neighbours, who became his vassals before he succeeded in wiping them out altogether, Jayavarman VII greatly extended the limits of his kingdom both to the north and to the east. It is worth noting that the name of the city of Siemreap, Angkor's present-day twin, signifies 'Conquered Siamese'. Chinese and Khmer historians claim that he also conquered part of Malaya and ventured right into the Burmese interior.

According to one stele, the king of Java, the 'two kings of Champa' and the 'king of the Yavanas' (in other words, the emperor of Annam, Long Can) all offered him ablutionary water, the supreme symbolic tribute. Was this just propaganda? A servile attempt to curry favour by members of his entourage or high-ranking temple officials? It is impossible to say. One thing is clear, however: in around AD 1200, the entire region that lay between India and China was dominated by a single ruler, and that ruler was Jayavarman VII.

George Coedès has studied the Angkor Thom statues and bas-reliefs in great detail. According to him, Jayavarman was a heavily built man with coarse features, who wore his hair pulled into a little chignon on the top of his head. As we have seen, the statue of the Leper King cannot have been modelled on Jayavarman, but did the king nevertheless suffer from that particular condition? Numerous bas-reliefs of the time depict the treatment of a nervous form of leprosy which doctors call 'cubital claw' and which is characterized by a violent contraction of the fingers. Given the extent to which a kind of royal tropism played its part in temple rituals and aesthetic considerations, it is tempting to wonder if the leprous patient in the bas-reliefs might in fact represent the king.

The Leper King has furnished the material for one of the most enduring myths in Khmer culture. Its source is perhaps to be found in a medieval Hindu text which describes how a Cambodian king suffering from leprosy went on a pilgrimage to the valley of the Ganges. And the fact that Jayavarman VII founded more than a hundred 'hospitals' might be regarded as a practical expression of the myth. Such charitable actions certainly demonstrate a serious preoccupation with illness and perhaps also, as George Coedès suggests, a concern 'to win credit and thereby alleviate his own misfortune'.

However serious a form his illness took, Jayavarman VII is nevertheless known to have reigned for almost forty years. He was still on the throne in 1201, when, a stele tells us, he dispatched an embassy to the court of Peking. He is thought to have died in around 1220, at the age of eighty or thereabouts. A devout Buddhist, he worshipped in particular the bodhisattva Lokesvara, in whose image he is represented in the Bayon, and at the time of his death he is said to have been 'on the path to the superior Enlightenment' which rules over the 'grove of the passions'. It is to this great conqueror and temple-builder that a maxim worthy of Marcus Aurelius is ascribed: 'The king does not suffer from his own ills but from those of his people.'

Standing at the centre of his capital, Angkor Thom, the Bayon is Jayavarman VII's masterpiece and the most elaborate expression of the Khmer genius. According to Paul Mus, it represents the cosmic mountain described in Indian cosmology, Mount Meru, which forms the axis of the world, vertically prolonged by a Meru that extends beneath the earth and the sea.

The royal cities of India are microcosms expressing, as Mus puts it, 'the dual power, secular and divine, radiating from the king's person and spreading across the earth'. The multiple image of the central shrine is the Buddhist symbol of the god-king, representing his dual identity as both god and king, and on top of the Bayon's towers Jayavarman is represented in the guise of the bodhisattva Lokesvara.

The four identical faces on each of the towers symbolize the royal power blessing the four points of the compass, as Mus explains. 'Each tower undoubtedly corresponds to one of the provinces of the kingdom, or, more precisely, to the religious and administrative centre of that province. Thus, if the four faces symbolize the royal power radiating across the kingdom, the fact that these faces are placed above each province's centre of worship – and, by allegorical extension, above the province itself – was perhaps intended to signify that Jayavarman VII was king of that particular province as he was of Angkor. Hence the necessity of building new towers with faces for each area of the kingdom over which he claimed sovereignty. Jayavarman's "great miracle"... was, above all else, the way he succeeded in extending the image of his administrative and religious power across the whole of Cambodia under a single sign – the portrait of himself as symbol of unity in diversity.'

No description of Angkor is complete without quoting the eloquent Chinese traveller Chou Ta-kuan, who accompanied a mission dispatched to Cambodia (or Chen-La, as it was known in Chinese) by the Middle Empire at the end of the thirteenth century, fifty years or so after Jayavarman VII's death. Chou Ta-kuan had a delightful knack for assembling all kinds of curious information, and the following is perhaps particularly worth noting: 'As for the golden tower inside the palace, it is here that the king goes to sleep each night. According to all the local people, the tower has a resident spirit, a serpent with nine heads, master of the earth and of the entire kingdom. Each night this spirit appears in the guise of a woman, with whom the king is obliged to couple. Even the king's wives keep out of the way then, frightened of the consequences of entering the tower while he is thus occupied. At the second watch, the king then leaves the tower and is at liberty to sleep with his wives and his concubines. Should the spirit fail to appear one night, however, this is a sign that the barbarian king is about to die.'

Barbarian? Of course, the subjects of the Son of Heaven regarded all non-Chinese as 'barbarians'. At a later date, travellers from Europe, whether monks or laymen, would be likewise designated (with the further specification 'southern').

Two hundred years later, a Capuchin friar from Portugal saw the Bayon 'in ruins', but still 'regally adorned', describing it as 'one of the most extraordinary temples, though incomplete'. But this Portuguese traveller also drew attention to a feature which seems not to have struck his Chinese predecessor, visiting the site three hundred and fifty years earlier: the country's extraordinary system of irrigation, its moats, canals, bridges, rivers and fountains. It was upon just such a water system that the abundance of rice, cattle, buffaloes and deer depended, another factor that appears to have amazed this old globe-trotter.

Two centuries later it was the turn of a young French diplomat, a companion of Ernest Doudart de Lagrée and member of the Scientific Commission of the Mekong, to enter the 'Siamese' province of Angkor. The dominant impression he came away with was one of 'dread'. Of the ancient city of Angkor Thom, he remarks, 'only the outer walls are still intact. The gates are guarded by fifty stone giants . . . interconnected by the coils of a monstrous snake. . . . Plunging into the dense jungle which fills the vast area enclosed by those proud walls, one's overriding feeling is not amazement – though one feels that too, certainly – but sadness. To reach what few ruins remain involves clambering through impenetrable thickets, and a compass is necessary in order not to lose one's way in this vast solitude inhabited only by wild animals which call to one another with hoarse echoing cries that sound like human moans.'

Angkor's visitors have spoken of power, of conflicts, symbols, magic and *Angst*; but what about beauty? It leaps out so forcefully from Marc Riboud's photographs that I hesitate to add my own few poor words to such powerfully, if discreetly, expressive images. Angkor Wat and Borobudur are the magnificent culmination of India's architectural genius, which reached its fullest flowering – as René Grousset has brilliantly demonstrated – beyond that country's political frontiers, a fact that has also been true for other great civilizations.

Angkor's beauty is also intrinsically Khmer, monumental in its proportions. It is the beauty of fast-running streams and the still waters of the Barays – all reminding us that the region was originally little more than a giant river and a vast lake, bordered by neighbouring seas – the beauty of trees and roots, of fantastic woody coils thick as giants' sinews, of a plant-life so vigorous it can only be compared to the great forests of the Amazon Basin.

The skulls embedded in blocks of stone are a reminder of the cost in human terms of erecting pyramids or ziggurats, in present as in past civilizations. And yet, the succession of tragedies Angkor has witnessed does nothing to diminish its beauty. This beauty is everywhere: in the watery greenness of the light, the harmonious lines of the Wat, the jumbled confusion of the temple-mountains, the heart-rending commotion of the Baphuon, the soaring rose-coloured stairways of Pre Rup.

The most fascinating, if also terrifying, aspect of Angkor is what can best be described as the epic union of Nature and Man, the violent tension between root and pick, shoot and sickle, movement and rest, energy and pressure, power and revolt. . . .

A little more than fifty years ago, the great aesthetician Elie Faure, stopping off at Angkor on his journey round the world, captured perhaps better than any of his predecessors the magical strangeness of Ta Prohm and Preah Khan. He describes the 'plant stalactites' gripping 'the temple in a frenzy of passion like the arms of some giant octopus. . . .' But was the passion love or hate? The dividing line was a fine one. If we regard the temple as the work of Prospero, then the incursions of the banyan and its powerful rival the kapok represent Caliban's outraged response.

The focus of this century, as it draws to a close, has shifted from violent ideological dialogue towards the great debate which sets Nature against Man, naturalism against humanism. Nowhere is this debate more eloquently expressed than here, in the leafy shadows of the Baphuon and Ta Prohm, the temple of Brahma, which seems as if it ought rather to be dedicated to many-armed Vishnu.

Many people have regretted the loss of the 'orgy' of unrestrained plant-life that made the most casual of Angkor's visitors feel like an intrepid explorer, as Charles Bouillevaux and Henri Mouhot felt hacking their way through the undergrowth in the middle of the last century, and as Pierre Loti himself felt. Let the stones, the *apsaras*, Siva and all the works of human genius perish, these people argue, so that the Panic powers of the jungle may reign unimpeded.

If the need arose, however, to close ranks against the adherents of the back-to-nature school, and defend the preservation of architectural masterpieces as harmoniously integrated as these into their natural surroundings, we would have no shortage of support. We would be ready vigorously to defend the work undertaken, between 1907 and 1967, by Commaille and Groslier, Parmentier and Marchal, and by others like them. Their aims were humble ones; they did not claim to be 'restoring' what they were simply seeking to preserve. And yet, they succeeded in salvaging not just the stone itself, not just the spirituality embodied within the stone, but, as Elie Faure has put it, 'that organic architecture which leads reason to a perception of unity'.

Such a 'perception of unity' lies at the very heart of Buddhism. How is it then that, despite the presence of the Buddha hovering here, despite the monks' saffron robes brushing the sacred stones as they walk patiently back and forth, despite the gentle gestures of the women with their coils of raven-black hair and the supple movements of the young boys, hips moulded by their clinging *sampots*, peace still eludes this place where plant and stone are now reconciled?

Images of Angkor at the time when the Khmer Rouge roamed between Banteay Srei and the western Mebon call to mind that bewildering duality so characteristic of the Khmer people, that contradiction between the message of the Enlightened One and the methodical madness of the murderers. How are the two to be understood? How can we reconcile the serene faces of the *tevodas* with the grimaces of Pol Pot's henchmen clubbing the faces of their living victims into a bloody pulp?

It is true, of course, that Christians slaughtered one another mercilessly in the time of Saint Francis of Assisi, and that in Gautama Siddhartha Buddha's native land – also the native land of Mahatma Gandhi – political power is often won by the sword. And yet, it is perhaps at Angkor, beneath Lokesvara's serene gaze, that the outrage strikes us most forcibly.

Angkor is coming back to life, and the images Marc Riboud has brought back from its great forest of stones inspire us with some hope. His photographs are beautiful, but not in a seductive or a dishonest way: they do nothing to disguise the dark forces constantly threatening Angkor from beyond its walls, and they truthfully reflect the place occupied by men and women here among the tombs and temples and the ever-encroaching jungle. Riboud's images, placed in context by Jean Boisselier and Madeleine Giteau's expert texts, re-create Angkor as it is here and now, living in the midst of a suspended tragedy.

JEAN LACOUTURE

24

41

A Buddhist Presence amidst the Gods

It was the Bayon's air of mystery rather than the benevolent serenity of the colossal faces carved on each of its temple-towers which most forcibly struck Europeans visiting Angkor during the second half of the nineteenth and the first few decades of the twentieth centuries. Angkor Wat had a classical beauty, but the Bayon's strange symbolism was not so readily accessible. Angkor Wat, that 'grandiose and magnificent monument' as it has been described, was physically easy to reach and sufficiently well maintained by the resident monks for the noble harmony of its proportions to be immediately apparent, even to the most ignorant observer. The case was quite different with the Bayon. This ruined temple was a secret and mysterious place, located in the heart of Angkor Thom, Angkor's ancient and long-deserted capital, and buried beneath a mass of jungle vegetation.

In 1901, after a three-day visit at the end of the rainy season, Pierre Loti, describing himself as a 'disenchanted impressionist', noted his reactions on first witnessing Angkor's strange architecture and the extraordinary way in which it blended with its natural surroundings. (His impressions were to be gathered together eleven years later in the book *Un Pèlerin d'Angkor*, An Angkor Pilgrim.) After a torrential downpour had forced him to take refuge 'next to a large pensive Buddha, sheltering beneath his thatched roof', he continued walking towards the Bayon, 'battling all the while with thorn-bushes and creepers that spread in all directions'. He was obliged, he tells us, to hack his way through to the temple with the help of a stick. As for the temple itself, the jungle closed in on it from all sides, smothering and crushing it, while an army of giant fig-trees finished off the work of destruction, pushing through the stones and climbing right up to the top of the towers, which served the topmost as pedestals. 'Before leaving,' Loti continues, 'I looked up at these towers looming over me, smothered in vegetation, and suddenly I started, overcome with a peculiar kind of fear, on seeing a frozen smile of giant proportions directed down at me ... and then I saw another smile, over on another section of wall ... and then another three, another five, another ten; they were everywhere, and giant eyes were observing me from all sides. . . . I had been told about these towers with four faces, but I had forgotten about them. . . . The masks sculpted high up there in the air are of such superhuman dimensions that it takes a moment to make them out. Beneath the great flat noses the mouths are smiling, and the eyelids are half-closed in a coyly feminine way. . . .'

The Bayon has long been cleared of its mantle of vegetation and today it is difficult to imagine how this bare and dilapidated temple looked at the beginning of this century. The impressions of casual visitors, however, remain an irrelevance, failing to grasp Angkor's essential quality. For what is fundamental here is the profound and age-old significance of the site, and especially of Angkor Wat and the Bayon, for an entire people whose morality is firmly based on the Buddha's 'Law', that law which the Buddha taught 'for the good of all beings'.

From the seventeenth century onwards, Angkor was regarded as the true centre of Buddhism, not only for Cambodia, but also for a large section of the Indochinese peninsula. (The evidence of this is widespread, much of it assembled by B.-P. Groslier in his book *Angkor et le Cambodge au XVIe Siècle*, Paris, 1958.)

One Father Chevreuil, sent on a mission to Champa by the Society of Foreign Missions in Paris, spent the years 1665 to 1670 in Cambodia. Although unable to visit Angkor in person, he was much impressed by what he heard about the place, going so far as to quote the various observations in a letter dated 1668. After emphasizing that the religion of Cambodia was identical to that practised in the kingdom of Siam, he goes on to say that eight days' walk out of Siam there is 'a very old and famous temple' called Onco (Angkor). This temple is as 'renowned among the Gentiles of five or six great Kingdoms' as is 'Rome in the Christian world'; it is here that 'their Doctors' reside and it is from this temple that 'they receive their oracles and decisions in matters of Religion'. The letter continues to the effect that 'the kingdoms of Siam, Pegu, Laos, Ternacerim and various others make Pilgrimages there despite the fact that they are at war'.

In 1923, Noël Péri devoted a lengthy article to a copy of a Japanese plan of Angkor Wat dated 1715, which had been discovered shortly before by a professor from Tokyo University. Apart from the fact that this plan is the oldest known for Angkor Wat – the original having necessarily been drawn up during the years 1623–36 – it also reveals the interest shown in the temple by the Japanese, who were at this time maintaining steady relations with Indochina. What is perhaps surprising, however, is that Angkor Wat has been identified with Jetavana, the famous monastery of Sravasti, which was offered to the Community and which the Buddha claimed to prefer to any other temple. At Jetavana he had his own private cell, the Gandhakuti, where the exact position of his bed was laid down by certain texts as one of the *Four Immutable Places* used by all buddhas, past, present and future. Other texts, Tibetan this time, solemnly affirm that the plans of the monastery had been drawn up by the gods of Tushita Heaven themselves. This last assertion may have found an echo in the legends regarding the divine origins of Angkor Wat's founder, which had been in circulation since the end of the thirteenth century.

We should bear in mind at this point that Siam (present-day Thailand) was once commonly located in Magadha, 'in southern India' [*sic*], and that the Mekong was regarded as 'the largest river in the whole of India'. Thus, an assimilation of Angkor Wat with Jetavana, although not attested locally, would have seemed plausible enough to pilgrims from distant countries, particularly since the 'transposition' of India's holy places to locations beyond its borders, particularly in South-East Asia, is an established and well-known fact. The extraordinary layout at Jetavana is not dissimilar to the equally remarkable arrangements at Angkor Wat, while Angkor Wat's iconography also calls to mind the richness and diversity of the library collections at the famous study centre at Kosala. The tradition of learning attached to Jetavana would appear to have been identical at all the monasteries bearing that name, whether the Jetavana founded towards the end of the third century at Anuradhapura, in Sri Lanka, or the temple of Jetavana in Bangkok – Wat Phra Chetuphon, better known by the name of Wat Po – which King Rama III (1824–1851) sought to turn into an 'encyclopaedia in stone', where all contemporary learning would be assembled. Now, as we gathered from Father Chevreuil, the learning of Angkor Wat's 'doctors' was a matter of great renown. The Japanese pilgrims' apparent confusion over the identity and location of Angkor Wat is much less surprising, therefore, than it might at first have seemed.

One question remains to be answered: how an originally Vishnuite foundation could have become the important Buddhist temple whose fame spread well beyond the borders of Cambodia itself. The answer, provided by various sixteenth- and seventeenth-century Khmer texts, is confirmed by a lengthy tradition and even by certain of the Buddhist scriptures.

Thanks to its classical arrangement and harmonious proportions, Angkor Wat, the 'city-monastery' founded by Suryavarman II (1113–c. 1150) – in other words the city which was to become a Buddhist monastery – marks the culmination of Khmer architecture. Angkor Wat was the last of the 'temple-mountains', built according to an architectural formula devised by Indravarman at Bakong less than two hundred and fifty years previously; but unlike its predecessors, which were all Sivaite foundations, Angkor Wat was of Vishnuite inspiration. Its iconography, inspired by the epic poems and legends associated with Vishnu-Krishna, displays an obvious syncretism, while the sovereign's posthumous name, Paramavishnuloka (he who resides in the 'World of Supreme Vishnu'), reveals the temple's true orientation.

A temple dedicated to Vishnu thus became the most important Buddhist Khmer monastery – without even undergoing an immediate change of name from Preah Pisnulok. This smooth transition from the cult of Vishnu to the religion of the Buddha, even if it only occurred after the site had probably been abandoned for rather more than a century, may strike us as surprising. It is nevertheless clearly attested by the so-called 'modern' inscriptions at Angkor Wat and by a number of texts dating from the sixteenth and seventeenth centuries. From these we learn that the Preah Pisnulok (or 'Holy Vishnuloka', a survival of its original name) was regarded as 'the meeting place of the *mahakshetr* gods, the all-powerful *brahmarshi*, the divine guardians and the bands of Fathers' (the five principal Brahmanic gods), of the 'great ascetics of the Brahman class', of protective deities often confused with local spirits and, finally, of the Manes.

This transformation of a temple which, even by name, remained predominantly Vishnuite into a Buddhist monastery of outstanding importance ought not in fact to surprise us. Mme Saveros Pou has emphasized the number of 'Buddhist elements in the *Ramakerti*', the Khmer version of the *Ramayana*, the most famous of the epic poems associated with Vishnu. Unlike its Indian counterpart, the *Ramakerti* traces the lineage of Ram (Rama) not only to Naray (Narayana, one of Vishnu's many names) but also to the buddhas.

It should be stressed that we are not dealing here with a mere fabrication by Khmer authors writing in the sixteenth and seventeenth centuries. The iconography of the Buddhist Khmer temple of Phimai, inspired by Mahayana Buddhism, borrows constantly from both Buddhist sources and the *Ramayana*; it dates from the early twelfth century. But we can go further: the *Ramakerti* explicitly refers to the canonical collection of the *Jataka*, or former 'Incarnations' of the Buddha. The *Dasaratha-Jataka* (No. 461), apparently narrated at Jetavana by the Buddha himself, differs markedly from the *Ramayana* and its various versions in that it neglects the essential elements of the epic – the kidnapping of Sita and the long struggle against Ravana and the Rakshasa. However, it does summarize the first books of the Vishnu poem and, in part also, the conclusion – the long exile of Ramapandida, his brother Lakkhana and Sita (here the sister and not the wife of Rama); Rama's life as a hermit; and finally the princes' return to their capital, followed by the coronation and reign of Rama. It is in the Pali text that we find the Buddhist slant which is the source of the *Ramakerti*'s originality and, in particular, this detail: Rama[pandida] 'was at that time the Bodhisattva' – he who at the end of his existences has become the all-knowing Buddha. The transition from an originally Vishnuite to a Buddhist orientation was henceforth an easy matter and we can better understand why the name Angkor Wat (Nagar Watt) only gradually came to replace that of Preah Pisnulok.

Angkor Thom and the Bayon form two inseparable parts of a single whole: the new capital built by Jayavarman VII (1181–*c.* 1218) on the site of the original city, which was founded by Yasovarman I (889–*c.* 900) and captured and desecrated by the Chams in 1177 following a surprise attack. Four years later, Jayavarman, having succeeded in ousting the occupying forces, had the memorable inscription already quoted by Jean Lacouture engraved on one of the four stelae erected at the inner corners of the city walls (see page 10).

The stele at the south-eastern corner of the walls bears the following inscription, continuing the description of the city in the guise of a young bride: 'Pure, thanks to her master's conduct [or: the conduct of Brhaspati, the planet Jupiter, but above all the chaplain of the gods, the god personifying piety and religion], possessing divine power, worthy of praise, containing the great [garden] Nandana, and having at her summit the [hall of] Sudharma of the [city of] Sudarsana, her domain was comparable to Heaven.' The name of the city, Sudarsana ('pleasing to look at'), and the references to the garden of Nandana and, in particular, the Sudharma ('good order' or 'justice', the name given to the assembly-hall of the gods) invariably call to mind the city of Indra, the abode of Indra and of the Trayastrimsa gods (the 'Thirty-Three' gods, on the summit of Mount Meru). Once we have made this connection, we have the key both to the architectural symbolism of Angkor Thom and to its royal founder's intentions. The detailed, and scarcely varying, descriptions of Indra's city in the Buddhist scriptures, both in Sanskrit and in Pali, explain precisely what lies behind the originality of Angkor Thom and the Bayon.

The city founded by Yasovarman I, and sacked by the Chams, needed much more than mere restoration: what was required was a whole new symbolism, and the capital had to be built afresh, but in a way that maintained links with the old city. It was not just the material ravages wrought by the invading Chams that necessitated the foundation of a new Yasodharapuri, but the collapse of the entire politico-religious system upon which Angkor's power had depended. All the institutions and rituals which, since the first half of the ninth century, had been aimed at safeguarding the independence and inviolability of the kingdom suddenly proved ineffective: the capture of Angkor by the Chams merely proved their futility. Simply repelling the invader would not be sufficient to restore the old order or to obliterate the consequences of defeat.

Jayavarman VII did much more than just liberate his kingdom from the invader: he discovered a means of reducing the Cham victory to an inconsequential episode that could have no further repercussions. Unlike his royal predecessors, Jayavarman was a Buddhist, an adherent of the Mahayana sect, and it was in Buddhist cosmology, in particular the legend of the victory of the gods, led by Indra, against the *asuras*, that he found the model which would enable him both to restore the Khmer kings to power and to build an 'impregnable' capital. The inscriptions dating from his reign are sufficiently explicit for us to be quite certain which texts served as guidelines for Angkor's reconstruction, and to be able to reject out of hand other more tentative or obviously flawed hypotheses on the subject.

The significance of Angkor Thom's architectural layout resides in the account of the battle between the *devas* and the *asuras*, particularly its conclusion. According to the great Phimeanakas inscription, the Khmer kingdom represents the world of the gods and the Chams represent the *asuras*: 'Jaya Indravarman, king of the Chams and as arrogant as the demon Ravana ... brought his army over in chariots and attacked the country of Kambu, which is like the Heavens. . . .' The Cham offensive against the Khmers was to end in disaster for the assailants, just as the *asuras*' attack on the divine city of Indra ended, after a short-lived victory due to the advantage of surprise, in a resounding defeat for the *asuras*. Moreover, Jayavarman was to provide his capital with an effective system of defence said to be identical with that installed by Indra in the divine city 'in order to prevent any new offensive on the part of the *asuras*'. The composition of this 'guard' is recorded, with slight variations, in both the Pali and the Sanskrit texts. As Mahayanists, the builders of Angkor Thom naturally drew their inspiration from the Sanskrit sources. These tell us that there are 'five [sorts of] guardians of the [Thirty-Three]. . . .' These are the *nagas*, 'who live on the water', the *yakshas*, who appear under various names, and the four 'Great Kings', regents of the four cardinal points. Alongside these guardians appeared 'images of Indra himself holding a thunderbolt in his hand'.

These details in the Sanskrit texts provided the inspiration for the magnificent composition decorating each of Angkor Thom's five gates and their approaches. Four of these gates mark the axes of the city walls, while the fifth, the Gateway of Victory, gave sole access to the royal palace. The gates each represent a tower with three summits and are crowned with the colossal faces of the four Great Kings, the guardians of the four points of the compass. The central passageway is guarded, in an equally original manner, by the 'images of Indra' mounted on the three-headed elephant Airavata, whose three trunks serve as corner supports.

Beyond the wide ditch that surrounds the outer walls, other striking figural compositions incorporating *nagas* and *yakshas* protect the routes into the city. It has been suggested that these figures towering over the road in the form of giant parapets represent the famous myth of the 'Churning of the Ocean'. However, the 'giants', who are holding on to the body of the *nagas* 'as if to prevent them from fleeing', would be doing the very opposite with the serpent's body, according to this interpretation. Such movement at the central pivot would be incompatible, moreover, with the notion of stability associated with the summit of Mount Meru and the divine city.

In the case of the Bayon, built in the centre of the city, the problem is more complex. Thanks to the inscription noted above, we know that it represents the Sudharma, the assembly-hall of the gods; but it is also the most important of Angkor's temple sites. Although not incompatible, these two functions are not clearly distinguished in the sources, and this duality complicates our understanding of the monument's architectural layout, contributing to the element of 'mystery' that has frequently been associated with the Bayon.

The Bayon is built at the heart of Angkor Thom's nine square kilometres (about three-and-a-half square miles). Its numerous shrines are enclosed within a galleried precinct measuring no more than 160 by 140 metres (525 by 460 feet), the effect of which is rather cramping. The actual harmony of the design can only be appreciated by an examination of the plan or, better still, if one has the opportunity, by flying over the site. An enormous circular central shrine is surrounded by radiating chapels, the whole complex occupying the centre of a cross inscribed inside a quadrilateral and suggesting a giant mandala or yantra. The temple may well have derived its name from the word 'yantra', Bay Yon being the pronunciation of Pa yan[tra], meaning 'father (or master) yantra'. It would appear that the Bayon, the last of Cambodia's 'temple-mountains', is simultaneously the earthly replica of the divine assembly-hall in the city of Indra and a kind of pantheon bringing together, around the image of the Buddha housed in the central shrine, the various gods worshipped throughout the kingdom alongside important figures from its history who have been granted posthumous honours (most of whose names appear in the temple inscriptions).

The bas-reliefs of the first- and second-floor galleries are in very poor condition and in many cases difficult to identify. Those on the second floor are mainly devoted to the legends of the gods and are of rather uneven workmanship. Those on the first floor, some of them unfinished, illustrate land and sea battles, military processions and scenes from daily life, providing a valuable source of information regarding Khmer society at the end of the twelfth century. Some experts have suggested that the battle scenes represent real historical battles between the Khmers and the Chams. This is almost certainly only partially correct. If, as seems likely, contemporary events were used here to illustrate scenes from ancient history or mythology, what we are actually dealing with is an illustration of the battles between the *devas* and the *asuras*. (Those battles, concluding with Indra's resounding victory, already provided the symbolism for Angkor Thom's gates.) It was no doubt regarded as more important to identify the career of Jayavarman VII, king of the Khmers, with that of Indra, king of the gods, than merely to commemorate a contemporary event.

Finally, we come to those colossal faces carved on each of the Bayon's shrines. Many people have, mistakenly, described them as smiling, and their eyelids as lowered, but if the faces occasionally appear this way, it is due merely to a trick of the light as it plays over the crumbling sandstone. Their expression is the typical expression of the Buddhist in the 'active state of mind' which the scriptures call *brahmavihara*, the 'things pleasing to Brahma', the 'sublime state' leading the mind to charity, compassion, joy and tranquillity. But what of the four-faced deity whom local people have traditionally identified as Brahma? This identification was widely accepted at first, and even adopted for the faces on Angkor Thom's gates, although these are in fact quite different. Later, a number of other hypotheses were advanced, and the one that finally met with unanimous approval was Paul Mus's suggestion that the deity in question was Avalokitesvara, whom Jayavarman VII is known to have worshipped. However, there are problems with this identification, too. No images of a four-faced Avalokitesvara are known to exist. Moreover, the bodhisattva is never shown wearing a warrior's head-dress, as here, nor do any of the sources attribute such a role to him. On the other hand, the texts describing the Sudharma tell us that it is here that the gods hold their 'Good Order' (Sudharma) assemblies under the chairmanship of Indra, that the Buddha comes down in his 'eternally youthful' aspect to honour each of the gods individually by his presence. To do this, Brahma comes in the guise of the chieftain Gandharva Pancasikha (which explains the warlike head-dress). Although none of these details appear in any known Mahayanist source, these sources do allude to the 'Good Order assemblies', and since there is no significant difference in cosmological matters between the Mahayanist and the Theravadan traditions, it seems most likely that the faces carved on the Bayon's towers belong to Brahma in the aspect of Gandharva Pancasikha.

As in the past, the crowds of pilgrims that come flocking to Angkor today are more inclined to worship the statues built near the Bayon, which are of more recent date, than those of the mysterious and now long-deserted temple. And yet the same air of serenity radiates from the faces of these humble pilgrims as from the colossal temple faces – that serenity which Buddhism imparts to all its followers.

JEAN BOISSELIER

Serenity, Sensuality

The stone faces were watching me, but the monks were oblivious of my presence. And yet the equipment slung over my shoulder betrayed my foreignness and branded me as a barbarian. I had grown used to the solitude of this forsaken place, but now an astonishing vision unfolded before my eyes: for three days and three nights, hundreds of monks and thousands of pilgrims gave voices to the silence of the ruins.

The beauty of the faces, the profiles of shaven heads and the folds of the monks' robes became a part of the very design and texture of the stone itself. The smiles for ever hovering at the top of each of the towers and the elegant voluptuousness of the *apsaras* belonged to the world of stone, the pilgrims' slow gestures as they performed their devotions or begged for alms belonged to that of the living; yet each mirrored the other in a scene announcing a serenity reborn. The eye was never more enchanted. Never was backdrop more majestic than in this realization of the harmony so passionately desired between nature, man and setting.

If my first impression was that of a chaotic mountain of stone and a randomly milling crowd, I soon perceived an ordered harmony in what lay before me, in this colossal geometry of stone blocks, hewn almost a thousand years previously, welcoming again a multitude of monks and pilgrims who had come together to honour the Buddha of their fathers.

The Buddha is everywhere, his image multiplied to north, south, east and west, on the towers of the Bayon, the most beautiful and at the same time the most strange of Angkor's temples, a temple-mountain with so many summits and towers that only archaeologists have bothered to count them. (There are, they say, fifty-two.) For my part,

I preferred to let my eye wander over the towers, and to experience the enchanted gaze, mirrored to infinity, of those colossal faces that look down through lowered lids – those faces commissioned by King Jayavarman VII and executed by an ingenious sculptor-architect whose name we shall never know.

In the crowd of worshippers, beautiful young women from Phnom Penh, their lacquered hair set off with a white flower, mingled with shaven-headed widows, young monks and sages who could have been either young or old. None had any idea what pleasure they were giving: unwittingly, like the delicately sensual *apsaras* on the bas-reliefs, they offered themselves up to my enjoyment, and I felt as if my eyes and my hands were caressing the stone, brushing against bodies and faces.

Angkor provides a feast for all the senses. As Elie Faure puts it, the Khmer sculptor gives everything 'we hear and taste and feel' a shape. 'He sculpts the whispers, glimmerings and scents of the forest, the rhythmic sound of marching troops, the deep cooing of birds anticipating love, the low growl of wild cats prowling through the undergrowth, the invisible current flowing through the nerves of dancing women as the music begins to throb and the sensuous rhythms increase.'

On the second day of the celebrations, a huge procession wound its way slowly around the Bayon with much chanting and burning of incense. There were a myriad banners and parasols spread beneath the age-old trees, and countless offerings to the gods, and silver dishes brimming with mangoes and papayas, pineapples and a thousand different kinds of flowers. It was a vision from a dream, so close to the scenes carved in stone. Since it is the photographer's constant obsession to get higher and higher for a better view, I ran ahead and overtook the procession, and, spotting an old tree-stump, I climbed up it in a couple of bounds. It was the ideal look-out: I had the whole spectacle unfolding before me, five hundred monks advancing directly into my field of vision. All of a sudden, however, I leapt into the air – not from excitement, but from shock: I had sat on a red ants' nest and was being bitten all over. In an attempt to rid myself of the creatures, I jerked my arms and legs about as if I had St Vitus's dance and tore off my shirt, while down below me the monks, previously withdrawn in silent contemplation, burst into peals of hearty laughter. I should have known that no one raises himself above the head of a living buddha without incurring the wrath of some god or other.

There is a story that, in 1912, Georges Méliès managed to climb to the top of one of the banyan trees that grow around the Bayon. From this vantage-point he was actually higher than any of the towers and was able to take a shot of the temple from above, something that no one had ever done before. Once he was on the ground again, he apparently asked the temple curators to cut down the tree so that no one else would ever be able to take the same photograph – a double insult which would surely not go unpunished by the gods.

The procession broke up and the pilgrims scattered among the columns of the Bayon, brightening the sober stone with a brilliant patchwork of colours: the red reserved for weddings, a variety of browns, the ochre and saffron of the monks' robes, the widows' white (the colour of mourning), the peasants' black, and finally the motley colours of the *nouveaux riches*, the merchants and managers. After the fanatical forced egalitarianism of the Pol Pot regime, when to possess a watch or a fountain-pen could be a capital offence, Khmers today are both able and eager to assert their individuality by the way they dress, the jewelry they wear and sometimes even the motorbike or car that they drive, the conspicuous addition of a flowered spare-tyre cover helping to draw attention to the prized possession. To display one's religion and one's devotion to the Buddha is also considered good form: Buddhism has now been reinstated as the national religion and its doctrines and rites no longer have to be taught or practised in secret.

There was to be a full moon that evening, and the thousands of pilgrims had assembled to consecrate one of the buddhas housed beneath a pagoda in the style more of an eastern Saint Sulpice than of Jayavarman VII. The monks were planting young trees brought from Bodgaya on the banks of the Ganges, where the Buddha attained Enlightenment two and a half thousand years ago.

Huge fires were lit to cook the rice for the communal meal. Overhead, banners shaped like crocodiles hung from bamboo poles so long and slender and supple that the slightest breeze made them bend. Stretched between the trees, among the Bayon's square columns, were hammocks – the traditional equipment, along with the mosquito-net, indispensable to any travelling Khmer.

At nightfall, a fire illuminated the sacred dancers performing on an improvised platform. Their bodies spangled with gold and silver, arms and legs bare, fingers splayed like spatulas, they set about imitating with fluid movements the thousand *apsaras* carved in the Bayon's and Angkor Wat's stone façades.

No one has described better than Bernard Groslier the sensuality of these 'divine dancers, two or three of them intertwined at once . . . the exquisite sweetness of their expressions, the rhythmic quality of their gestures, the whimsical charm of their braided hairstyles and of their gilded tiaras. Dreamlike creatures, for whom one almost feels one has the courage to deserve the heaven where they cavort and dance.' When he saw the most beautiful of all Khmer nudes, on display at the Musée Guimet in Paris, Groslier was entranced by the sensuousness of 'this torso opening like a flower of flesh from the slender stem of a skirt creased with light. . . . We can still feel the hand that shaped it, caressing it lovingly, coming back again and again to the full curves, the silky incline of the hip. Flesh vibrant, sensual and pure as one would wish embraces to be.'

I met Groslier on arriving at Angkor in 1968. It was to prove an invaluable initiation. Shy and painfully aware of my own ignorance, I felt even more awkward than usual in the presence of this reserved man. At the time I first met him, he was running his hand over a carved wooden beam, a relic of Angkor Thom. Wood that has survived nine centuries was a rarity, he told me. My eyes, meanwhile, were attracted to the mural depicting a vast royal procession, which covered the entire wall. Then Groslier suddenly started talking in an animated way about Banteay Srei. He told me how it had first been dated to the fourteenth century, its construction thus considerably postdating that of Angkor Wat, but how the date had subsequently been shifted to the tenth century thanks to the information provided on a stele. How were we to explain such sophistication at such an early date, he asked, and proceeded to answer the question himself with a distinct note of pride in his voice: 'We've just discovered the key: the king who built this temple with all its lacy pink sandstone preferred young monks to those heavenly dancers.' One wonders how many other mysteries his combination of passion and erudition has cast light upon.

André Malraux expressed a poor opinion of archaeologists in *The Royal Way*, and in his later *The Voices of Silence* he qualifies anyone who only appreciates 'the specifically plastic qualities of the works of the past [as] a superior type of modern barbarian'. It is true that knowing their history and the stories attached to them can only help us to appreciate Angkor's wonders all the more readily.

Although he never visited the East, the sculptor Auguste Rodin fell in love with the classical Khmer dancers who toured France in the twenties. He claimed to be captivated by 'their strange and marvellous seductiveness' and followed them from Paris to Marseilles, producing some splendid drawings.

The French historian René Grousset, having once declared that 'in the whole of Far Eastern art there is not a single representation that comes anywhere near our *Pietàs*', nevertheless changed his mind under the influence of Khmer art. It succeeds, he said, in giving to Buddhism that quality which had as yet eluded Indian sculptors: 'the inner smile, the smile with closed eyes, floating, elusive, the smile of the buddha or bodhisattva savouring in his heart the peace that is Nirvana'.

Elie Faure, René Grousset and Bernard Groslier all had a tendency to view the perspectives and symmetry of Angkor's architectural plans in terms of seventeeth-century French classicism. But these three scholars, all of them great writers, brought up in the rigorous cultural tradition of Judaeo-Christianity, shared – at a few years' distance – the same sense of amazement at the sensuality of Khmer sculpture, the fullness and roundness of whose forms, seeming to inhabit a Paradise before the Fall, were, for them, a sheer revelation.

A stele found at Angkor celebrates this sensuality in the most lush terms and is a paean to the glory of visual splendours. It reads: 'Drawn by the flower of its glory to the fruit of the beauty of the mango-tree of her body, the bee of the eye of men could nevermore tear itself away.'

In the thirteenth century, long before Faure, Grousset and Groslier's time, another traveller, an elderly Chinese of a more prosaic disposition, Chou Ta-kuan, travelled across Cambodia, recording for posterity everything he saw in 'this kingdom of barbarians'. Chou Ta-kuan, who was part of an ambassadorial mission, was enchanted by this country 'where clothes are not necessary, where rice is easy to buy, women are easy to come by, the houses easy to furnish, and business easy to manage. . . .' He even passes on such details as the fact that the men wash with their left hand and eat with their right.

If Chou Ta-kuan were to return to Angkor today, would he see a great many changes? The ox-drawn carts are the same, their wheels have the same number of spokes, the boats the same curvature, the fishermen the same nets, the dancers the same movements, and the same music is still in fashion. There is here a permanence of things, a continuity: the friezes in the Bayon and at Angkor Wat reveal everyday scenes from a golden age which are mirrored still in daily life.

Who built these temples, these mountains of stone? An old Cambodian once said to me: 'They weren't men who built them – they would have had to be giants. They were gods.' The Khmers have good reason to believe in their divine builders, in those divinities too who, twice a year, reverse the course of the river that links the Mekong with the great lake of Tonle Sap. This 'reversal of the waters' seems indeed something of a miracle, just like the raising of blocks of sandstone weighing several tons to the top of the Bayon's towers.

What was the reason for building them? According to Buddhist doctrine, a follower of the Buddha has to earn 'merits'. The eighth-century Chinese sage Tong-pin thus noted down on going to bed one night: 'Saved the life of a butterfly, earned a merit.' King Jayavarman VII, after building the most beautiful of temples and draining his kingdom dry, might well have written in his journal in the evening of his life: 'Built the Bayon, earned a merit.'

I love the romanticism of the forest and of the roots spreading like a pitiless tide over the fallen temples. If Piranesi is said to have been the architect of ruins, dreams and the fantastic, by such a definition he might also have been the architect of Ta Prohm and Ta Som, which look like cathedrals sunk beneath the waves. You have to wander through this submarine world of hanging creepers and nightmarish roots in the shape of octopuses and snakes, 'this maze of galleries and courts with no way out', plunged in the immense solitude of time, to understand how the treasures of an entire civilization almost disappeared for ever. Generation after generation, wave after wave of banyan and silk-cotton trees have pushed aside and overturned these massive blocks of stone with the slow thrust of their sap. The roots which entwine and envelop the stones seem to maintain a precarious balance. But when the tree dies, the tower collapses.

Once it had razed the wooden cities and palaces, the forest laid siege to the stone temples. They fought the encircling jungle with incredible resilience. But after five centuries of siege they weakened abruptly, like a garrison on the point of surrender. It was then that the French archaeologists stepped in and lifted the siege.

We know about the folly of those kings, the builders of temples whose colossal dimensions and ornamental excesses have never been surpassed. But the epic task of restoration, lasting more than a century, was a work of almost equally gigantic proportions – and just as necessary a folly.

MARC RIBOUD

Captions to the Photographs

17 Causeway giant at one of Angkor's gates (1990)

This statue, now eroded and festooned with lichen, is said to represent the hunter Kukhan, prince of the forest, from the *Ramakerti*, the Khmer version of the *Ramayana*, which notes: 'And this Kukhan was huge and powerful. He was so massive and shaggy-haired that he looked like a mountain.'

18–19 Preah Khan

To the north of Angkor Thom stands the huge temple of Preah Khan, whose name signifies 'the Sacred Sword'. It was at one time a city called Jayacri: in 1191, 'at the place, bathed with his enemy's blood, where he [Jayavarman VII] had won victory [Jayacri] in battle, he founded a city bearing the same name. Its stones and its golden lotuses altered the colour of the earth, and it still glistens today as if it were smeared with blood' (Preah Khan stele, Angkor).

20–21 Ta Prohm

A fig-tree, possibly hundreds of years old, whose vast, swollen roots are growing down over a temple roof, trailing over the archways like giant tentacles, to bury themselves in the rock beneath.

22–23 Roots of a kapok tree

The tree roots pour over the roofs, tumbling in all directions like a flow of lava, sometimes breaking the stones apart, sometimes holding them together. Here and there, the jungle 'respects a façade, frames a row of columns without destroying it. And, in places, it even cements together with its powerful creepers a porch that was on the point of collapsing, props up a crumbling archway and grasps pillars or an entablature in its strong arms...' (Guy de Pourtalès, *Nous à qui rien n'appartient*, 1931).

24 Preah Khan

A root as sinuous as a creeper has framed the image of a *devata* and trails down her arm like one of those garlands of jasmine buds which frequently adorn the shoulders of the young goddesses who guard the temple doors.

25 One of the four faces on a tower at Ta Som (1969)

Guy de Pourtalès notes 'the broad and powerful face whose features have scarcely evolved in seven or eight hundred years....'

26–27 Ta Prohm

Jayavarman VII built the temple of Ta Prohm in 1186 and had a statue erected in honour of his mother as the goddess of Supreme Wisdom, a divinity of Mahayana Buddhism. According to Maurice Glaize, '16,640 people lived inside the walls, 13 of whom were high priests, and 2,740 officiants, of whom 615 were dancers... 3,140 villages and 79,365 people were employed in the service of the temple.' The contents of the temple included '5 tons of gold tableware, 512 silk beds and 523 parasols' (*Les Monuments du Groupe d'Angkor*, 1948).

28–29 Preah Khan

The vaulted roof of this gallery has collapsed in an avalanche of stone, and tree roots cascade down over the ruins, but a group of gods, as if oblivious of the devastation, continue to join their hands in a gesture of worship on the façade of one of the shrines.

30–31 Ta Prohm

A kapok tree has knocked over a balustrade and spread its giant roots in all directions as if in an attempt to block the entrance. Henri Mouhot was deeply disturbed by the sight of all these monuments gradually being destroyed by the jungle. He comments: 'The work of destruction continues even against those that are still standing, imposing and majestic, alongside the piles of rubble' (*Voyage dans les Royaumes de Siam, de Cambodge, de Laos...*, 1868).

33 Trees among the ruins

In front of a giant fig-tree, whose twisted roots worm their way between the stones, a *sralao* trunk rises up straight as a pillar, slightly fluted and covered in little dark patches where the bark has peeled back. The date carved on the trunk, originally 1963, has been retouched to look like 1863.

34–35 Preah Khan

This kapok tree's giant knotted roots look like the limbs of some fantastic creeping animal whose supple trunk has already knocked over the vaulted archway in its path. They slither towards two pillars which rise up very straight, as if to protect the two impassive gods housed beneath the coping of the wall.

36–37 Ta Prohm (1990)

In the hollow of a tree, perching behind a root, villagers have placed two plaster skulls next to some half-burnt sticks of incense and some pieces of red cloth, the remains of a ceremonial rite – a macabre little grouping which reminds us of the piles of skulls found in the grave-pits of the Khmer Rouge.

38–39 Causeway giant, Preah Khan

As at Angkor Thom, giants holding the body of a *naga* look down from either side of the long causeways leading into Preah Khan. The leprous patches of lichen eating away the faces of this multi-headed giant give it an even more forbidding expression, appropriate to its role as guardian of the city.

40 Ta Prohm

This piece of dead wood looks a little like the head of an angry dragon that is about to breathe fire.

41 Face-tower, Ta Som (1968)

The four faces over the entrance to the temple of Ta Som once seemed to come alive as sunlight flickered through the leaves of this fig-tree and played over their features. Today, the tree is dead and the expression on the faces remains fixed.

42 Preah Khan

Roots of all shapes and sizes have wrapped themselves around these blocks of stone and grasp them like tightly bound cords as if to hold them in place. The atmosphere of the temple would be oppressive if the leaves rustling in the wind and glinting in the sunlight did not add a life of their own to the scene.

43 Ta Prohm

Here, where the temple roofs have fallen in completely, leaving nothing but a pile of giant rubble free from invading vegetation, it seems a pity that this young villager has hacked even the wild grasses back with his machete.

44–45 Ta Prohm

Near a roadside pavilion, a gallery has collapsed, exposing a corbelled vault. The intrados is made up of tiered sandstone blocks crowned with a single large slab, while the stones of the extrados have been cut in a curve to give the impression of a barrel vault. Khmer architects preferred corbelled vaults to true vaults, perhaps in accordance with an Indian saying, quoted by Henri Parmentier, that 'voussoir vaults never rest, only corbelled vaults sleep'.

46 Ta Prohm

A dead root coils along the top of a wall, looking like a giant snake.

47 Face-tower at the temple entrance, Ta Som (1969)

The faces still look the same as they did in Pierre Loti's day – he visited Cambodia in 1901 – with 'roots draping their foreheads like strands of ancient hair' (*Un Pèlerin d'Angkor*, 1912).

48 Ta Prohm

Another root winds its way between the blocks of sandstone like one of those snakes which Pierre Loti observed sliding among the ruins: 'Our footsteps fall softly in the grass and all we hear is the discreet slithering of snakes.'

49 Cruciform courtyard, Preah Khan

The Hall of Dancers, as it is called, is shaped like a cross and consists of four small courtyards. The friezes of 'remarkably elegant and finely executed' *apsaras*, or heavenly dancers, running over the passageways confirm for Maurice Glaize 'the probable use of this location as a room for ritual dancing'.

50–51 The Bayon (1990)

This young monk, whose yellow robe creates a bright splash against the grey stone, ignores the smiling goddess who, for eight hundred years, has guarded the threshold he is about to cross.

52–53 The Bayon (1990)

According to the Vinaya, one of the rules governing Buddhist monastic life, Buddhist monks are not allowed to eat between noon and daybreak, although they may take non-alcoholic drinks during this period, and also smoke cigarettes – like the young monk in the centre of the picture.

54–55 The Bayon (1990)

These two monks are strolling round the temple in the early morning. The younger of the two has covered his freshly shaved head with a corner of his robe, and each of them has a bag slung over his shoulder in which he keeps his few personal belongings and whatever alms he has received.

56 The Prah Ngok (1990)

The huge statue of the Buddha known as the Prah Ngok is seen here through a doorway in the Bayon. In 1990, a three-day festival took place in honour of this sacred image. Erected in the sixteenth or seventeenth century, the Prah Ngok Buddha has been restored on many occasions and has been coated in cement and repainted.

57 Monks collecting alms near the Prah Ngok (1990)

The monks advance in a long line, their yellow robes shimmering in the sunlight and their shaven heads shining like bronze. Until recently, it was customary for monks to receive only gifts of food, the donors pouring a little rice into their begging bowl (thereby earning themselves merits), but nowadays, since begging is no longer allowed on a daily basis, monks may also accept banknotes, which are deposited in the metal lid of their begging bowl.

58–59 Monks having a meal in the Bayon's outer gallery (1990)

The monks are eating off mats spread on the paving-stones by fellow Buddhists, some of whom also serve them, while others sit on their haunches and watch, their hands joined in a gesture of worship.

60–61 The Bayon (1990)

In a small room in the Bayon, two monks set about the complicated task of draping their robes around themselves. Called the *uttarasanga*, the robe is made from cotton and varies in colour from saffron to nasturtium-yellow. On the right, a man with a shaven head is rolling between his fingers a cigar made of *sangker* leaves. Over his white jacket, he has draped a grey and red cotton plaid scarf, the *krama* worn by Cambodian peasants. He may be an *acarya*, a former monk turned layman who knows how to perform the religious rites.

62–63 The Bayon (1990)

A group of monks chat to some laymen. A bas-relief behind them shows figures seated in a palace gallery watching a procession of wild animals, including deer, rhinoceros and large birds.

65 Young monk near the Siemreap river

Guy de Pourtalès might have been describing this very same monk when he noted: 'All at once, I saw Cambodia embodied in the person of a monk. He had stopped at the side of the road . . . his head was shaved and his shoulders and legs were bare, and he looked us square in the face, with an expression devoid of curiosity, but full of thoughtfulness. . . .'

66–67 Monks in a gallery in the Bayon (1990)

The two young monks in the foreground, to judge by their age and their shy expressions, are almost certainly *samanera* or novices, while their elder counterparts are fully trained monks, or *bhikkhu*. Again, Guy de Pourtalès could have been speaking of faces such as these when he remarked: 'I immediately recognized the Khmer of the statues, his thick, well-defined lips, the prominent line of his brow ridge and his slightly flattened nose. . . .'

68–69 Monk in front of a bas-relief in the Bayon (1990)

Chou Ta-kuan, who visited Cambodia in 1292, noted that the monks 'shave their heads and wear yellow clothing, with the right shoulder bared; as for the lower part of the body, they knot a skirt of cotton cloth around themselves and go barefoot.' None of this has changed since his time.

70–71 The Prah Ngok (1990)

During the 1990 festival, the monks spent three days and three nights in the vicinity of the Bayon, taking part in the ceremonies during the day and sleeping on mats on the ground at night. Behind the statue, mosquito-nets have been hung from random attachments.

72 Buddhist encampment near the Bayon (1990)

Families came from all over Cambodia to take part in the festival, the inhabitants of neighbouring villages and of the nearby town of Siemreap arriving either by bicycle or in trailers towed by motorcyclists, those from farther afield travelling for the most part by boat across the Great Lake, since the roads were badly damaged during the war and were unsafe to use.

73 Near the Bayon (1990)

One of the celebrants at the three-day festival, almost certainly a monk, has set up his quarters a little way away from the Prah Ngok, draping his mosquito-net over a monk's parasol and attaching it to the trunks of two sugar-palms, or *thnot*. On waking in the morning, the first thing he would see would be the Bayon's towers and its central shrine rising from the upper terrace.

74 Temporary home in a corner of the Bayon's outer gallery (1990)

This family has taken advantage of one of the galleries' small corner rooms to set up more intimate accommodation away from the main encampments. The hammocks and mosquito-nets, which they have slung between the pillars, are indispensable pieces of equipment for all Khmer travellers.

75 Counting alms, the Bayon (1990)

Once the donations have been collected, one of the monks is responsible for counting the money and dividing it up for distribution to the various monasteries. This particular monk is being helped by a child, almost certainly one of the young disciples who receive instruction from him in addition to taking part in joint religious exercises. According to their scriptures, Buddhist monks are not strictly allowed to handle money, but since collecting alms on a daily basis is currently forbidden, they are in fact obliged to collect and distribute donations in order to protect the livelihood of the community.

76 The Bayon (1990)

Squatting on the debris of a corner pavilion, two monks smoke and chat while waiting for the next ceremony to begin.

77 The Bayon (1990)

This woman's shaven head and white shawl (white being the colour of mourning) indicate that she is a widow. Carved on the pillars behind her are groups of *apsaras*, or heavenly dancers.

78 Siesta time near the Bayon (1990)

This little girl is the granddaughter of the man in the hammock.

79 Prohibition notice, Angkor Wat (1990)

At the entrance to Angkor Wat, a notice lists the various activities that are prohibited in the temple grounds. These include: making a hole in the trunk of a *cheuteal* tree and building a fire in it as a means of extracting resin; riding a bicycle or driving a car into the temple; letting off rifle shots to frighten away wild animals; allowing cows or buffaloes to wander among the monuments; photographing the monuments; growing rice in the sacred pools; impeding irrigation by opening or closing the valves of the fresh-water reservoirs.

80 Peasant on the road out of Angkor Thom

This row of benevolent giants lines the road out of Angkor Thom. The peasant walking alongside them is carrying grain for threshing. He has adopted a traditional technique of walking, with long, rhythmical strides, to balance the two baskets slung over his shoulder, and typifies the body build described by Guy de Pourtalès: 'undernourished but healthy... covered in the firm flesh that is the result of steady labour... narrow-hipped but with the broad shoulders typical of the Asiatic frame'.

81 Causeway giant at one of Angkor Thom's gates

This giant's nose is broken, his cheek chipped, and his face disfigured by patches of pale lichen, but his expression has lost none of the solemnity that attaches to his role as one of the divine guardians of the city. Note the jewelled headdress, which reveals his divine status.

82 Causeway giant, Angkor Thom

Yet another of Angkor Thom's guardians, this mutilated giant holds a *naga* above the ditch and glowers fiercely down at the passers-by.

83 The Bayon's upper terrace

This man is squatting in front of a face on one of the towers, relaxing and gazing at the central shrine with its extraordinary crowning architecture. The people of Cambodia are proud of their country's past and eager to talk about Angkor's former glory.

84 The Bayon's inner courtyard (1990)

The Japanese-made shirts worn by these two teenagers, printed with the image of a motorbike, represent only too clearly the intrusion of the modern world, with its noise and emphasis on speed, into the traditional life of Cambodia, symbolized by this silent temple whose active life has ceased but whose peaceful atmosphere still encourages contemplation.

85 One of the entrances to the Baphuon (1990)

One of these young men has lost a leg, the other both legs, as a result of exploding mines. After twenty years of war, this country has produced many such casualties, and the child, pretending to limp while leaning on two bamboo sticks, is simply imitating what has become a commonplace sight.

86 Terrace at Preah Palilay (1990)

This temple is named after the forest of Parileyyaka, where the Buddha lived for a time as a recluse, fed and served by an elephant and a monkey. The temple fronts on to a beautiful terrace constructed in the style of Angkor Wat and guarded by two *dvarapalas* (entrance guardians), two lions and two *nagas*, whose bodies originally formed a balustrade.

87 Angkor Wat

This woman is sitting at the foot of the stairs leading to the gallery of bas-reliefs. She has shaved her head, probably in fulfilment of a vow, and is wearing a red- and grey-checked *krama* and a patterned sarong whose predominant colours are dark red and yellow.

88 Prasat Kravan

Prasat Kravan's five tower-shrines were built towards the middle of the tenth century and restored at the end of the 1960s.

89 The banks of the Siemreap (1990)

A woman wearing a sarong is crouching on a wooden beam washing the piece of material she has just worn to take a bath. The peaceful life of the river has resumed, the life of another age, little changed from that depicted on some of the Bayon's bas-reliefs. Up until 1975, *norias* (bucket wheels) turned in the stream with a mournful creaking which mingled, in the evening, with the harsh rattle of the cicadas, but dams have slowed the river's current and it is now too sluggish for the *norias* to be able to turn.

90–91 Angkor Wat

This lion and *naga*, now badly damaged, guard the entrance steps at the western end of the temple. In front of them, two Khmer women are resting and refreshing themselves with mangoes after climbing the stairs to the central shrine to worship the images of the Buddha. Over the years, Angkor Wat has never ceased to attract pilgrims, as the numerous inscriptions testify.

92–93 The Angkor Wat moats (1969)

Until 1970, the moats at Angkor Wat formed an impressive stretch of water, in which villagers from neighbouring hamlets came to bathe – an occupation which has always been of central importance in the daily life of the Khmers. As Chou Ta-kuan notes, 'The country is terribly hot and one cannot get through the day without bathing several times.... In some cases, each family has a pool, in others three or four families share one, and everyone, male and female, goes in naked. Only when the father or mother or some elderly persons are in the pool do the sons and daughters wait their turn.... But for persons of the same age there is no obstacle to their entering the pool together. They simply hide their genitals with their left hand as they enter the water.'

94–95 Steps at the western entrance to Angkor Wat (1969)

Many visitors, both Khmers and foreigners, have succumbed to the temptation to leave evidence of their visit by scrawling graffiti on the temple monuments. For many years, one of the pillars in Angkor Wat's central shrine displayed the name of a ship, the *Bouclier*, whose crew visited Angkor at the end of the nineteenth century. In 1969, various graffiti, including the year and some Japanese characters, were scrawled on the breast of this lion. These last graffiti had disappeared in 1990, but the lion still bore the name of a legionnaire from Marseilles named Sauveur and the date of his visit, 1946.

96 *Devatas* in the cruciform courtyard at Angkor Wat

Only the *devatas* of Angkor Wat are represented in groups. The one to the right of the picture wears a diadem and gilded flowers and a broad necklace decorated with pendants. Her companions wear their hair knotted in whimsical styles and a chain with a heavy ring dangling between their breasts. The artist's models were young girls from noble families, the one to the right of the picture being dressed in the style of a princess or lady of the court, the other three in an earlier style, with the hair decorations and jewelry of feudal princesses.

97 *Devata* at the western entrances, Angkor Wat

This *devata* may perhaps recall some of the feminine features described in the *Satra Kakey*, a poem by King Angduong, which relates: 'The beauty of the king's first wife, his precious Kakey, was faultless. No other woman could compare with her.... She was miraculously born from a *karnika* flower. Her beautiful face resembled the full moon; her hair was shimmering black silk; her brow shone like red gold; her smile was exquisite; her voice was sweet; her cheeks had the delicate freshness of fruit; her fine nose seemed to have been drawn by a consummate artist; her teeth gleamed like pearls; her black eyebrows formed a perfect curve; her bright eyes sparkled. She had lovely shoulders, divine hands, supple little fingers and pearly nails. Her firm breasts were like flowers just beginning to open; she had graceful hips and feet like golden bananas.'

98–99 *Devatas* at the western entrances, Angkor Wat

Angkor Wat's finest and most ornate *devatas* are located at the temple's western entrances, among them these princesses in the courtyard of King Suryavarman II, depicted on a bas-relief which is said to be 'historical'. The same emphasis on ornate decoration is found in a Khmer story, where a queen is described as wearing 'gorgeous fabrics embroidered with gold flowers. Her wrists and ankles were ringed with gold bracelets set with diamonds, and she was crowned with a diadem of fine gold set with so many precious stones that it glittered like sunlight. On her fingers were numerous precious rings' (Story of Neang Mornah Meadea).

100–1 Close-up of two *devatas* at Angkor Wat

These two *devatas* exude a subtle sensuality and might be compared to the ladies at the court of Ravana, who, in the *Ramakerti*, are 'as beautiful as the *apsaras* of Tavatimsa heaven. Some of them hold lotuses. They . . . wear gold amaryllises at their ears and necklaces of flowers. . . . They have slim waists and breasts rounded like golden apples.'

102–3 The Churning of the Ocean, bas-relief, Angkor Wat

This bas-relief depicts a variety of marine creatures swimming about in a turbulent sea, which the gods and their enemies, the *asuras*, are in the process of 'churning' as a means of extracting from it the elixir of immortal life. Some, like the serpent-*naga* in the centre of the relief, are mythical creatures. Others are representations of real animals from the Cambodian fauna. In the centre foreground, the large fish facing downwards are probably *trei damrei*, or elephant fish; the shoal of fish swimming behind are probably *trei pruol*, a type of large fish which are caught for drying; while, tumbling about to the left and right are four crocodiles, creatures whose presence the Chinese missionary Chou Ta-kuan had noted at the end of the thirteenth century: 'There are crocodiles as big as boats, four-footed animals that look in every way like dragons, but without the horns; their bellies are quite crusty.'

105 *Devata*, close-up, Banteay Srei (1969)

The heavy ear-rings, necklace free of pendants and garlands of pearls slung beneath the belt are decorative elements typical of the Banteay Srei style which subsequently disappeared, but this *devata*'s combination of elegance and sensuality is very much in the Khmer tradition. The novelist André Malraux was so enchanted by the Banteay Srei *devatas* that he could not resist taking a couple of them home with him, as he recounts in *The Royal Way*.

106 Causeway giant, Preah Khan

This giant's head, badly eroded and smothered with lichen, has lost much of the ferocity of its original expression. The crown of leaves marks him out as a warrior god.

107 Gallery of bas-reliefs, Angkor Wat (1990)

The shadow of a soldier armed with a Chinese sub-machine-gun (note the curved magazine) is reflected against a bas-relief depicting the final battle in the Indian epic the *Mahabharata*.

108–9 The Bayon

In 1177, the Chams, inhabitants of the coast of what is now Vietnam, fought a successful offensive against the kingdom of Angkor. The future King Jayavarman VII took the initiative and succeeded in repelling the invader, and his victorious battles are represented on the bas-reliefs of the Bayon's eastern and southern outer galleries. In the centre of this picture, arrows are flying around two Cham chieftains mounted on elephants, while, in the foreground, short-haired Khmer soldiers are fighting against Cham warriors wearing strange helmets shaped like inverted flowers.

110–11 Causeway giants at one of Angkor Thom's gates

The Chinese traveller Chou Ta-kuan notes: 'The city walls are approximately twenty *li* [just under seven miles] in circumference. The city has five gates.... Beyond the wall there is a deep ditch, and beyond the ditch are access roads provided with great bridges. On either side of the bridges there are fifty-four stone spirits, like generals, gigantic, terrifying.... The parapets of the bridges are made of stone and are carved in the shape of a snake with nine heads. The fifty-four spirits grasp hold of the snake, as if to prevent it from escaping.'

112 Upper terrace, the Bayon

Framed in an opening at the far side of a dark passageway is one of the four faces on one of the Bayon's fifty-one tower-shrines.

113 The Bayon

Francis Garnier, who visited Cambodia in 1866, describes just such a view as this: 'There are two levels of galleries superimposed one on top of the other, the lower level being so dark, and the manner in which the perpendicular corridors intersect being so complicated, that it is almost impossible to find one's bearings in this labyrinth and it becomes necessary to climb up to the higher terrace in order to gain a better perspective on the rest of the monument. From here, the view is astonishing: innumerable towers rise up on all sides, varying in height and circumference, and carved on the front of the towers are huge human faces turning towards the four points of the compass' (*Voyage en Indochine*, 1885).

114–15 Faces on the towers of the upper terrace, the Bayon

'I looked up at those towers looming over me, smothered in vegetation, and suddenly I started, overcome with a peculiar kind of fear, on seeing a frozen smile of giant proportions directed down at me ... and then I saw another smile, over on another section of wall ... and then another three, another five, another ten; they were everywhere, and giant eyes were observing me from all sides ...' (Pierre Loti).

116–17 Bas-relief in the eastern outer gallery, the Bayon

Peasants driving ox-drawn wagons are depicted alongside an army on the march. Their function was probably to supply and service the troops. In the centre of the picture, a woman carrying a wicker basket on her head turns towards a man, possibly her husband, who is driving a team of oxen. Behind him, a soldier is brandishing his shield.

118–19 The Bayon

The entrances, with their triple passageways and small dark rooms, create an atmosphere of mystery through which the visitor must pass in order to reach the upper terrace and to see the face-towers rising up on all sides. Francis Garnier expresses his unbounded admiration for this architecture, which he describes as 'skilful and original in its conception, severe in its geometric forms, and elegant in its details'.

120 Face on a tower, the Bayon

This face, carved on dressed sandstone blocks, has the typical features associated with the art of the Bayon: square jaw and thick, well-defined lips turned up at the corners in a half-smile. Louis Delaporte comments: 'There is in these slightly strange faces, whose features are nevertheless almost unvarying, a half-smiling air of strength and serenity, which has a nobility all of its own' (*Voyage au Cambodge*, 1880). In assembling the stone blocks, the builders aligned them more or less symmetrically, rather than staggering the joins, with the result that over the years huge vertical fissures have appeared between them, as can be seen in this close-up.

121 The Bayon

Every decorative element in Khmer sculpture has symbolic significance. While the garland of flowers held by the young goddess and the plant motifs are auspicious, the two monsters' heads concealed among the foliage assist in safeguarding the temple.

122–23 Great Causeway and western entrances, Angkor

'And there is the great avenue, running away into the distance, straight and sure . . . between the dark clumps of bushes wafting scents of jasmine and tuberose. Slowly, aimlessly, I begin wandering over the paving stones, leaving the temple behind me, hearing now only snatches of the monks' chanting as it gradually fades out, behind me, in the infinite silence' (Pierre Loti).

124–25 Corner pavilion of the Bayon's outer gallery

Pillars have collapsed and cracked, ceilings have fallen in, piers and architraves lie scattered on the ground, and yet, stripped of vegetation, the ruins reveal the astonishingly classical character of this architecture. 'Almost everywhere, vaults gape open to the sky, peristyles collapse, and columns lean in different directions, many lying broken on the ground' (Francis Garnier).

126–27 Baksei Chamkrong

Not far from Angkor Thom stands the temple of Baksei Chamkrong, 'the temple of the Bird which protects the city', seen here in the early-morning light. The surrounding forest is still full of shadows, its dense foliage glinting in the first rays of the sun, and the tall trunks of the *cheuteal* glow in the rose and tawny light reflected from the temple's brick shrine and the high stepped pyramid of laterite blocks on which it stands.

By the same photographer

1959 *Women of Japan*, André Deutsch, London

1964 *Le Bon Usage du Monde*, Editions Rencontre, Lausanne

1966 *Les Trois Bannières de la Chine*, Robert Laffont, Paris (English edition: *The Three Banners of China*, Collier-Macmillan, London, and Macmillan, New York)

1970 *Face of North Vietnam*, Holt, Rinehart and Winston, New York

1972 *Bangkok*, Weatherhill/Serasia, New York

1980 *Chine, Instantanés de Voyage*, Arthaud, Paris

1983 *Gares et Trains*, ACE Editions, Paris

1986 *Marc Riboud. Journal*, Denoël, Paris

1989 *Le Grand Louvre, du Donjon à la Pyramide*, Hatier, Paris

1989 *Marc Riboud*, Photopoche CNP, Paris (English edition, 1991: Thames and Hudson, London, and Pantheon, New York)

1989 *Huang Shan*, Arthaud, Paris

Afterword

Ever since seeing the photographs of Ernst Haas in 1956, I have been haunted by these temples buried in the jungle of Cambodia.

This book is the product of several visits. The first, in 1968, was for a publisher friend of mine, Nigel Cameron, with a view to producing an album that was in fact never completed. Two other visits followed in 1969, prior to the outbreak of hostilities provoked by the overthrow of Prince Sihanouk and the escalation of the Vietnam war.

My fourth visit, in 1981, followed the defeat of the Khmer Rouge by Vietnamese troops, and it was with the greatest pleasure that my wife and I were escorted on a guided tour through the ruins by Bernard Groslier's former assistant and faithful disciple, Pich Keo, who had succeeded in evading the clutches of the Pol Pot regime and was now the curator of Angkor.

My last and lengthiest visit, organized by Xavier Roze and Kek Galabru, was in 1990. The majority of the photographs in this book, and in particular those of the pilgrimage to the Bayon and the three-day festival, were taken during that visit. On that occasion, I had a young assistant, Florent de La Tullaye, whose help proved invaluable.

I cannot end this book without remembering those fellow photographers, in particular Gilles Caron, who fell victims to Pol Pot. For a long time, we searched for them and waited for them, but, though they came very close, they were never to see Angkor. We will never forget them.

MARC RIBOUD

The photographs in this book were taken with Leica cameras and Leitz lenses on Kodak and Ilford film. The original prints were made by the Publimod' et Imaginoir laboratories on Ilford paper. My particular thanks go to Patrick Consani, who was responsible for the majority of the prints.